For our favorite Little Seminole, Kohlton James.

~Jolee and Charity

FLORIDA STATE®

A
BC's

Jolee & Charity Sanborn

A Alumni Center

Bobby Bowden Statue

NAL CHAMPIONS

C

Chop

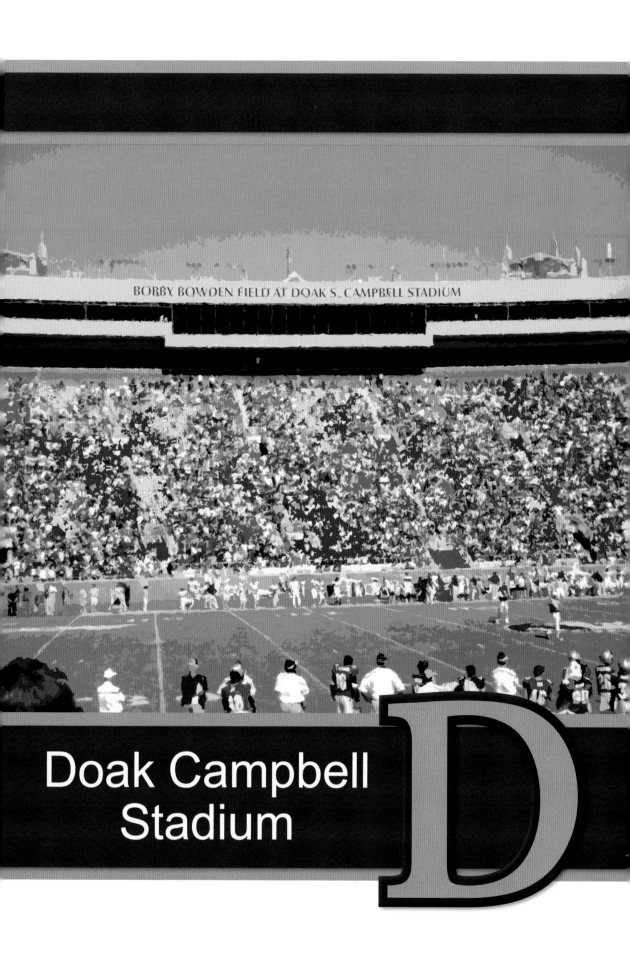

BOBBY BOWDEN FIELD AT DOAK S. CAMPBELL STADIUM

Doak Campbell Stadium

E

Eppes Statue

Flying High
Circus

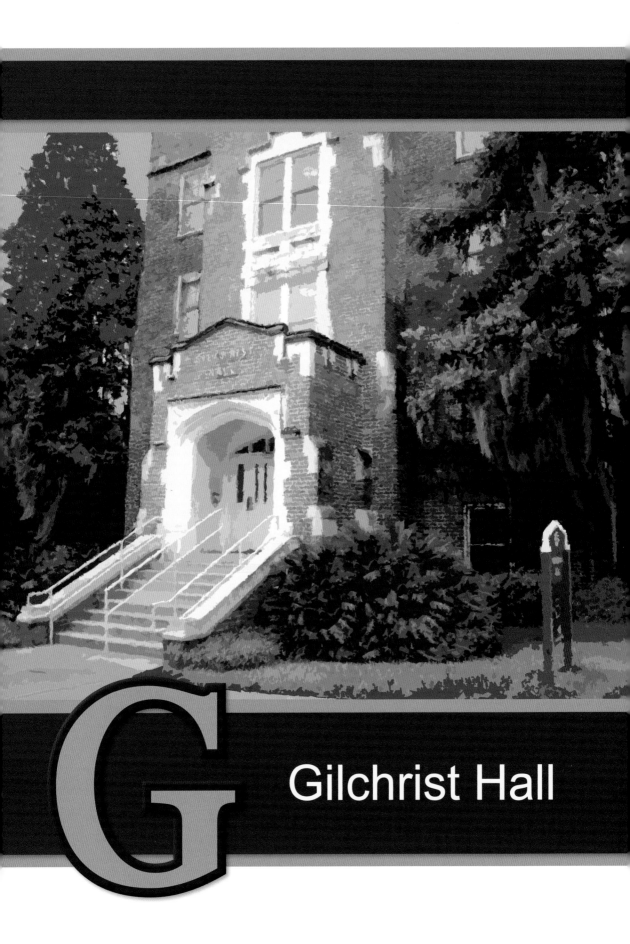

G

Gilchrist Hall

Howser Stadium

Integration Statue

Campus Map

2008

Journey Through
Campus

J

K Keeping the
Greek Tradition

Landis Green

M

Moore Auditorium

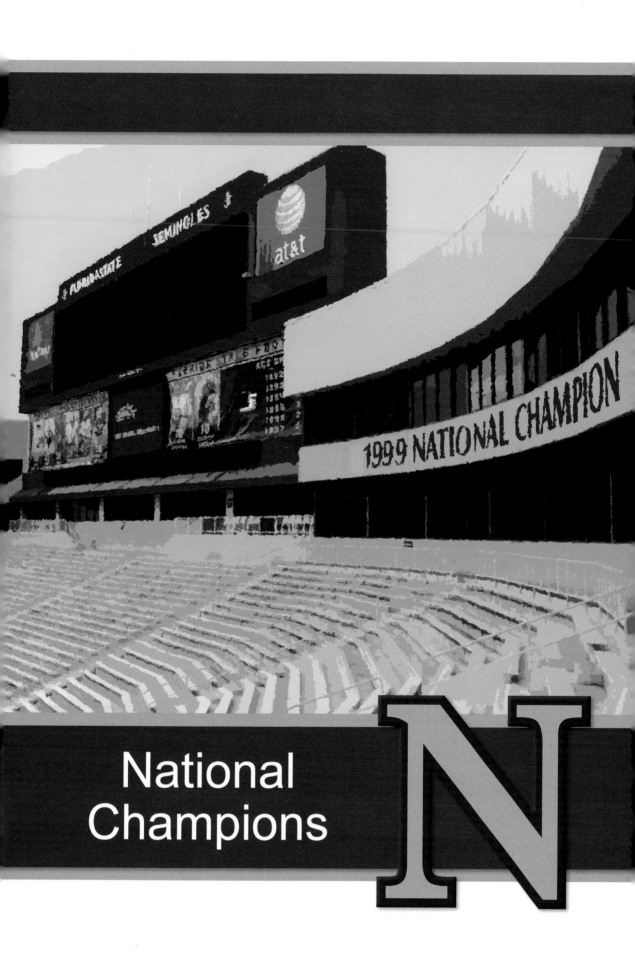

National Champions

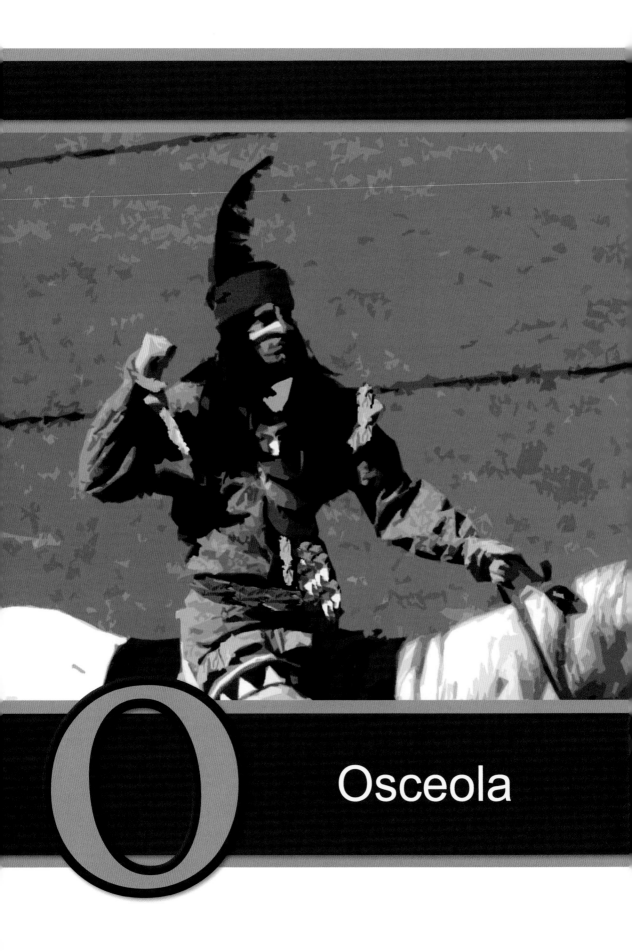

Osceola

Psychology
Department

Q

Quarterback

Renegade

R

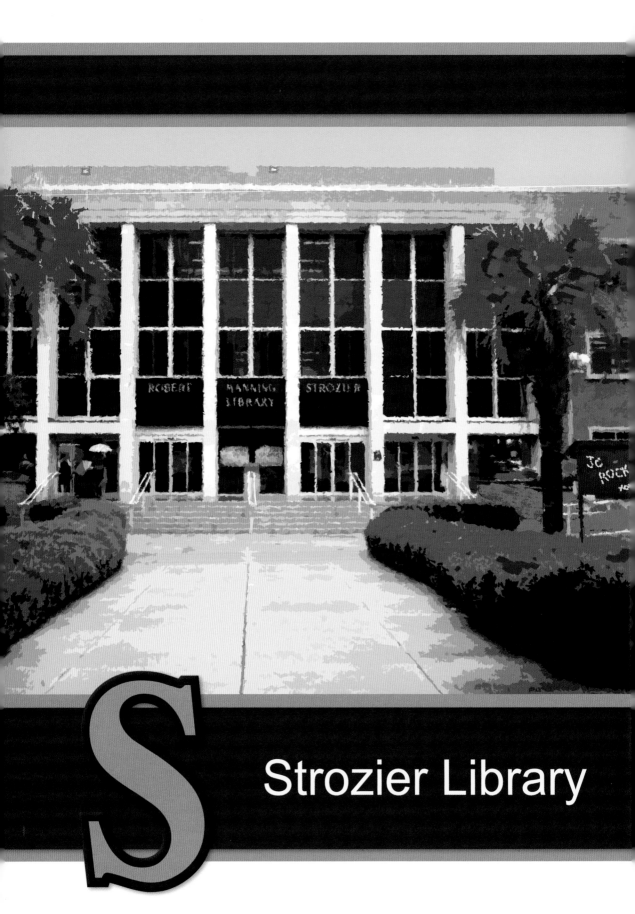

Strozier Library

Torches

T

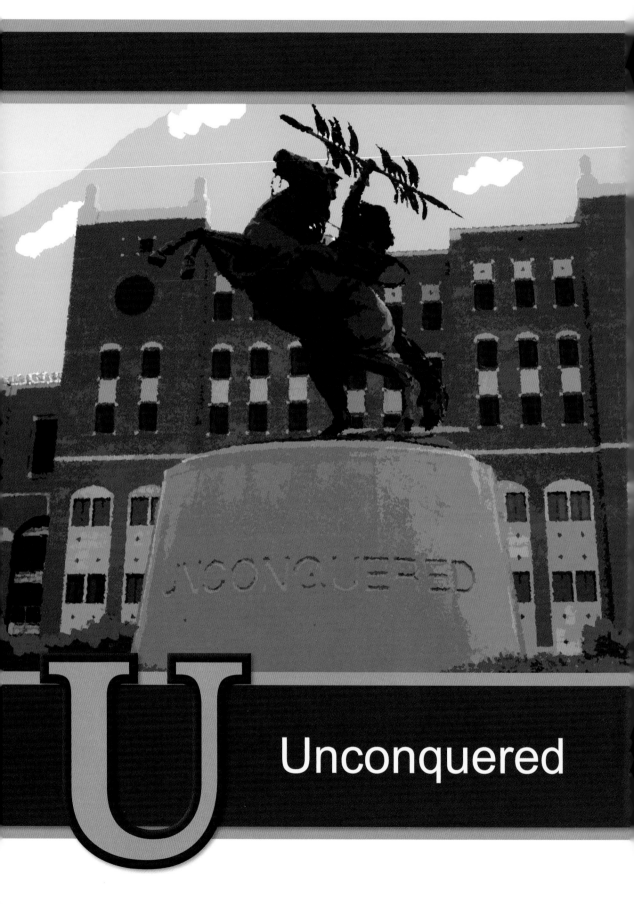

Unconquered

FSView

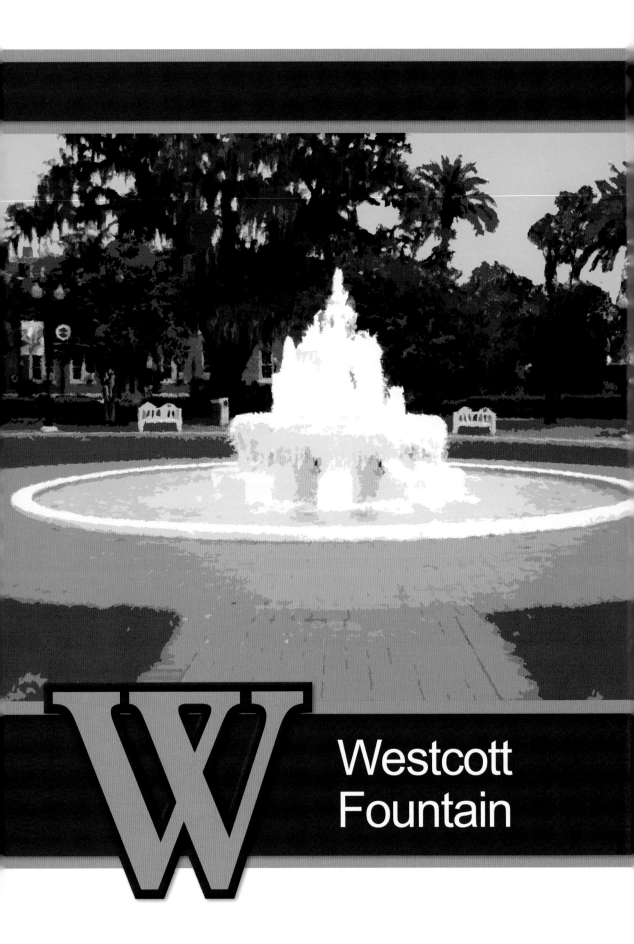

Westcott
Fountain

"X-ing" Out the Opponent

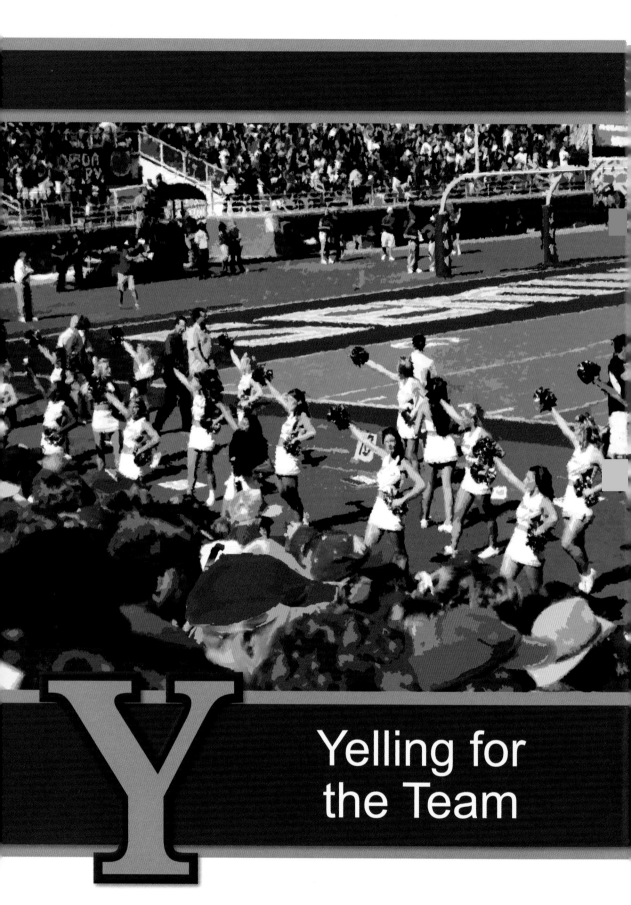

Y

Yelling for the Team

Zip-a-dee-doo-dah!

LOVE this book? Look for more ABC books from our collection focusing on YOUR favorite university's campus.

www.campuskidsbooks.com